MW00605755

DOGS
The family we choose

Every once in a while, a dog enters your life
and changes everything.

Melanie Steele
Photography by Holli Murphy

Lydia Inglett Ltd. Publishing
Award-winning publishers of elegant books

To Alba,

Whose unfailing strength of being and gentle spirit
gave tremendous meaning to my life.
I loved you more than life itself.

- MS

This book would not have been possible without Holli Murphy's generosity and talented eye for a dog, as well as Lindsay Cameron's patience, and uncanny relationships with all of our canine subjects. Nor would we have made it through the photo shoots or the composition of photos and text without Kathryn O'Connor's remarkable organizational skills and attention to detail. I owe them all a huge debt of gratitude. - MS

Dogs, The family we choose
ISBN: 978-1-938417-32-0

Published by Lydia Inglett Ltd. Publishing
www.lydiainglett.com
www.starbooks.biz
301 Central Ave. #181
Hilton Head Island, SC 29926
info@starbooks.biz

Printed in China.

Lydia Inglett Ltd. Publishing
Award-winning publishers of elegant books

"Everything I know, I learned from dogs."

– NORA ROBERTS

FOREWORD

Dogs make the world go 'round. Well, at least they do for me, and so many of my family members, friends, and neighbors. I grew up with dogs. They were more than just our pets—they were our companions, protectors and, on the ranch, our helpers. They did their chores with joy and never complained about being sent out to round up more mares or cows or to chase off the coyotes.

Today, my husband and I have the joy of bringing up a Hungarian Vizsla named Jasper. He is our second Vizsla, and we're nuts about him. Jasper doesn't have to do any work since we live in New York City (unless you count stalking the squirrels and pigeons as a job ...) Fortunately, for several weeks of the year, we get to take Jasper to our favorite place in the world—Palmetto Bluff in South Carolina. He doesn't have to work there either—unless you count sitting on the porch and lifting his head when someone rides by on their bike.

It was Jasper who pulled us toward a dog named Grady at a Crab Cake Social one night in Palmetto Bluff. And from there, we made more friends than we ever imagined. Good friends. With good dogs.

It is a joy to be a part of the community, and to be asked to participate in this important fund-raising book project that will further the research capabilities of Dr. Denis Marcelllin-Little and the important work he and his team conduct at the North Carolina College of Veterinary Medicine.

A final note—one particular marvel is how animal caretakers, especially veterinarians, care for our pets. Imagine going to a doctor and not being able to communicate what is wrong with you, why you're feeling bad or are experiencing pain. It would seem impossible for a doctor to be able to figure it out without any clues. And yet animal doctors do so every day. They've learned to read an animal's eyes and posture, and, it seems, they have a sixth sense to diagnose an illness and the suggested remedies to make it better. May we keep all those who care for our pets in mind and in our prayers—without them helping us take good care of our furry family members, our worlds might stop turning.

I hope that you will continue to support this project by giving *Dogs, The family we choose* as a gift."

– Dana Perino

Fox News Contributor and Co-host of *The Five*. Former White House Press Secretary, George W. Bush administration including at the Department of Justice after the terrorist attacks on 9/11. Perino lives in New York and South Carolina with her husband, Peter McMahon, and their dog, Jasper.

"A dog is the only thing that can
mend a crack in your broken heart."
– JUDY DESMOND

PREFACE

I am honored to share a few thoughts with you to celebrate *Dogs, The family we choose.* Dogs and people have developed bonds over many centuries. Dogs once hunted with people, but as homes of various shapes and sizes were built they were used to protect those homes and all therein. Our awareness of the importance and complexity of the bond between humans and animals has only increased since then.

Today we realize how important dogs are to our lives. The companionship they provide every day allows us to be more relaxed, confident and joyful. Dogs protect us, comfort us and help us through physical struggles, including therapeutic recovery and service assistance for the disabled.

To balance all the things that dogs do for us, we do our best to give back to them. Caring for dogs includes providing the best medical care for dogs suffering from diseases and injuries. It also includes conducting responsible research into their injuries and diseases to improve their lives.

Thanks to the generosity of the author, proceeds from the sale of this book will benefit the medical care and responsible research performed by our orthopedic group at the College of Veterinary Medicine at North Carolina State University in Raleigh, NC. Through clinical research begun in the 1980's, we have developed hip replacement methods, identified and described conditions that interrupt blood supply to the bone and affect bone formation, and investigated long-term impact of orthopedic procedures on these animals. This and other highly complicated but highly effective work continues, and this book will help further new research in those areas. For that, I am extremely thankful.

I know you'll enjoy this book. The photographs in it are wonderful reminders of the joys that dogs bring to our lives.

– Denis J. Marcellin-Little, DEDV
Professor, Orthopedic Surgery
College of Veterinary Medicine
North Carolina State University

WHAT IS IT ABOUT OUR DOGS?

Often the most beloved members of our families are the ones with four legs. Their appeal lies in the fact they are universally uncritical. They have an unrelenting love that has charmed everyone from presidents to paupers. Fala, Liberty, Millie and Buddy—we know them as well as their owners because of their own unique personalities.

My own experience began with my great-uncle's Weimaraner, a dog who was not only man's best friend but also a young girl's. When my husband and I married, we owned two Weimaraners before getting our first Greyhound. That Greyhound turned out to be the one that set us on a path towards breeding champion dogs and winning national competitions.

Along the way we have owned dogs with undying devotion and continually pleasant temperaments. There is truly no downside to their companionship—each errant bark or unexpected nip at the heels is just part of the learning process. We have opened our hearts to these animals and welcomed them into our homes.

When we made Palmetto Bluff our home several years ago we were met with fellow homeowners just as devoted to our four-legged companions as were we. At home among the winding roads and live oaks, we found that dogs were just as welcome to enjoy the natural beauty as anyone else. Instead of reluctance to dog breeders, we found neighbors who were supporters and enthusiasts.

That enthusiasm certainly comes through in the pages of this book. Their support—and yours, through this purchase—celebrates the positive experiences only associated with being a dog owner.

By donating the proceeds to the NC State College of Veterinary Medicine, we are ensuring a bright future for both dogs and humans. We share a similar genetic makeup with our companions, and the translational research being conducted at NC State will benefit all creatures in their ability to fight disease.

Because they enrich our lives so much, we all want our dogs to live their lives extensively and to the best of their ability. They are, simply put, the family we choose, and their health and happiness runs harmoniously with our own. Few choices ever turn out so well, and the dogs featured in the following pages certainly bring a new, yet familiar spark to each day.

That spark comes through in the photographs, and I hope you enjoy them as much as we did putting this book together.

– Melanie Steele

8

"If there are no dogs in Heaven,
then when I die I want to go where they went."
– WILL ROGERS

"What counts is not necessarily the size of the dog in the fight; it's the size of the fight in the dog."

– DWIGHT D. EISENHOWER

"The eyes are the mirror of the soul."
– WLADIMIR KLITSCHKO

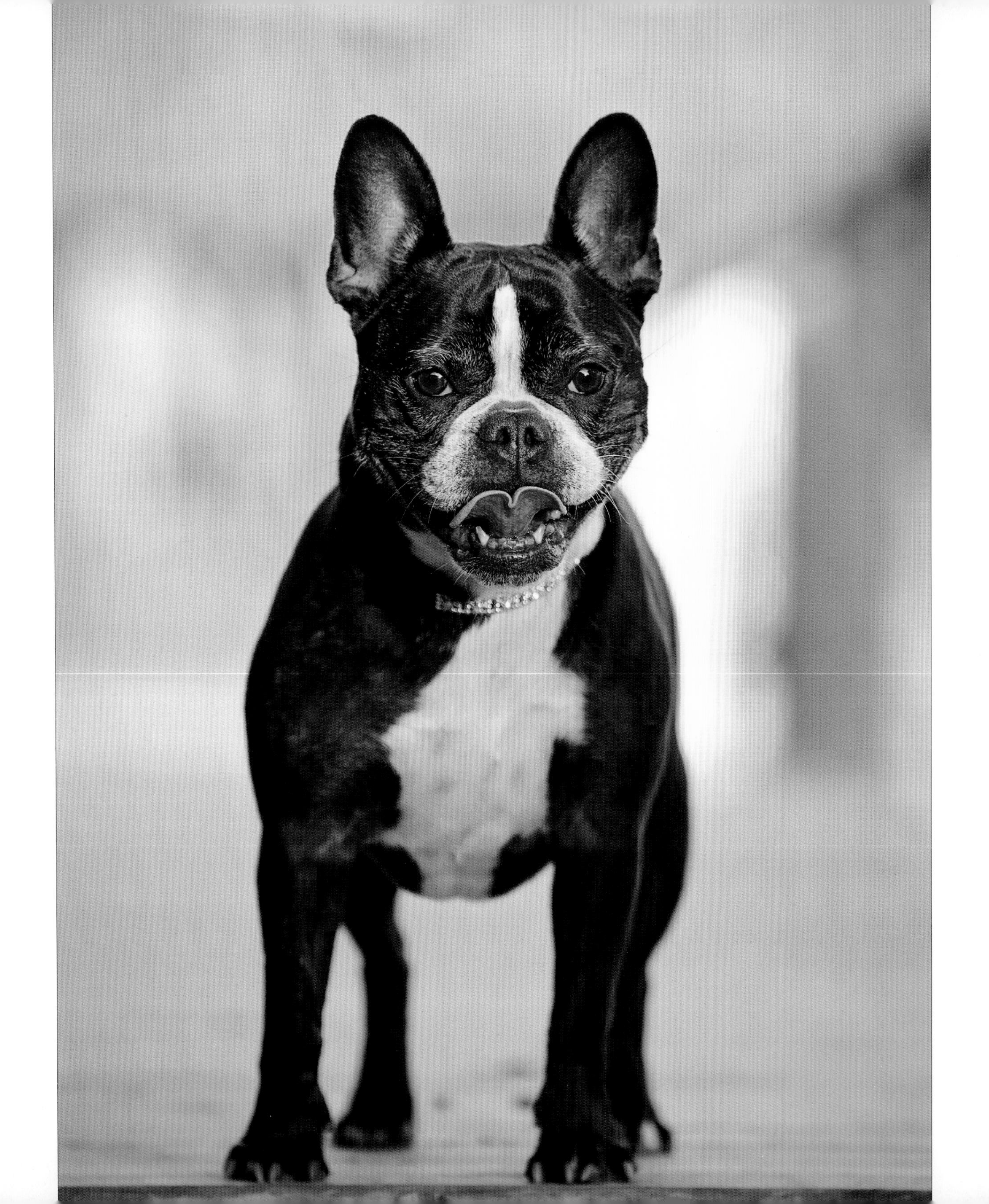

"Why does watching a dog be a dog fill one with happiness?"

– JONATHAN SAFRAN FOER, AUTHOR

"The dog is the God of frolic."
– HENRY WARD BEECHER

"I know that dogs are pack animals, but it is difficult to imagine a pack of standard poodles ... and if there was such a thing as a pack of standard poodles, where would they rove to? Bloomingdale's?"

– YVONNE CLIFFORD, AMERICAN ACTRESS

"When the Man waked up he said, 'What is Wild Dog doing here?'
And the Woman said, 'His name is not Wild Dog any more,
but the First Friend, because he will be our friend
for always and always and always.'"

– RUDYARD KIPLING, AUTHOR, "THE JUNGLE BOOK"

CHATHAM STEEL 20 MI
Vancouver
MOSCOW 5362 MILES
Mexico City 1436 Miles
GUATEMALA 2616 MI

"It's no coincidence that
man's best friend cannot talk."

– AUTHOR UNKNOWN

“To err is human,
to forgive, canine.”

– AUTHOR UNKNOWN

"The reason a dog has so many friends is that he wags his tail instead of his tongue."

– ANONYMOUS

"God said I need somebody strong enough to pull sleds and find bombs, yet gentle enough to love babies and lead the blind ... So, God made a dog."
– AUTHOR UNKNOWN

"Do not take life too seriously. You will never get out of it alive."

– ELBERT HUBBARD

"Be yourself.
Everyone else is taken."

– OSCAR WILDE

"I'm suspicious of people who don't like dogs, but I trust a dog when it doesn't like a person."

– BILL MURRAY

PALMETTO BLUFF
EST.
2014
SHOOTING CLUB

"They motivate us
to play, be affectionate,
seek adventure,
and be loyal."

– TOM HAYDEN

"Thorns may hurt you, men desert you,
Sunlight turn to fog;
but you're never friendless ever,
if you have a dog."
– DOUGLAS MALLOCK

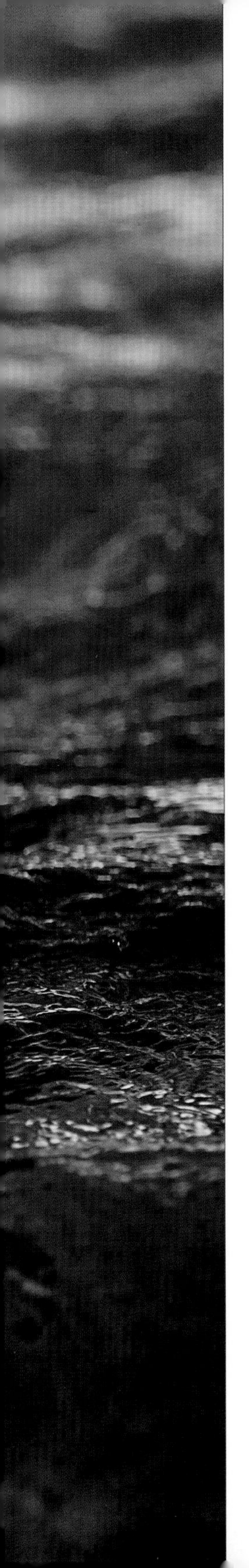

THE BLESSING OF THE ANIMALS

"Will, may you be blessed in the Name of the Father,
and of the Son, and of the Holy Spirit,
and may you and Jack enjoy life together
and find joy with God who created you."

– THE REVEREND JASON N. COLLINS

9

Jasper
American
Dog

"Dogs are not our whole life
but they make our lives whole."
– ROGER CARAS

"An animal's eyes
have the power to speak
a great language."

– MARTIN BUBER

"I can't think of anything that brings me closer to tears than when my old dog—completely exhausted after a hard day in the field—limps away from her nice spot in front of the fire and comes over to where I'm sitting and puts her head in my lap, a paw over my knee, and closes her eyes, and goes back to sleep. I don't know what I've done to deserve this kind of a friend."

– GENE HILL

"Some things just fill
our heart without trying."
– AUTHOR UNKNOWN

"By blood a king,
in heart a clown."
– ALFRED LORD TENNYSON

"Properly trained, a man can be dog's best friend."

– COREY FORD

"While he has not, in my hearing, spoken the English language, he makes it perfectly plain that he understands. And he uses his ears, tail, eyebrows, various rumbles and grunts, the slant of his great cold nose or a succession of heart rending sighs to get his meaning across."

—JEAN LITTLE

JOHN DEERE

"Friendship isn't about whom
you have known the longest ...
it's about who came and
never left your side."
– AUTHOR UNKNOWN

15-2680

CHEVROLET APACHE
CHEVROLET

“I can resist everything except temptation.”

– OSCAR WILDE

S18-12-15-6PB

"There is nothing truer in this world than the love of a good dog."

– MIRA GRANT

"One reason a dog can be
such a comfort when you're
feeling blue, is that he
doesn't try to find out why."
– AUTHOR UNKNOWN

"Dogs got personality.
Personality goes a long way."

– QUENTIN TARANTINO

"I think dogs are
the most amazing creatures;
they give unconditional love.
For me, they are the role
model for being alive."

– GILDA RADNER, COMEDIENNE

"No great mind has
ever existed without
a touch of madness."

– TOM HAYDEN

"I have found that when
you are deeply troubled,
there are things you get
from the silent, devoted
companionship of a dog
that you can get from
no other source."
– DORIS DAY

"Be sure to put your feet in the right place, then stand firm."

– ABE LINCOLN

"Some of our greatest historical and artistic treasures we place with curators in museums, others we take for walks."

– ROGER CARAS

JACK DANIEL'S
LYNCHBURG. TENNESSFE

"Everything I need to know I learned from my dog—
When loved ones come home, always run to greet them. Never pass up the opportunity to go for a joyride.
Allow the experience of fresh air in your face to be pure ecstasy."

– AUTHOR UNKNOWN

"There is no psychiatrist in the world like a puppy licking your face."

– BEN WILLIAMS

"As long as I keep on aging I am pretty
lucky. Not everyone has
the opportunity to grow old."
– CAMERON DIAZ

"Until one has loved an animal, a part of one's soul remains unawakened."

– ANATOLE FRANCE

"Ever consider what our dogs must think of us? I mean, here we come back from the grocery store with the most amazing haul—chicken, pork, half a cow. They must think we're the greatest hunters on earth!"

– ANN TYLER

"A greyhound should be headed like a snake,
And necked like a drake,
Footed like a cat,
Tailed like a rat,
Backed like a beam,
Sided like a bream."

– FROM THE BOOK OF ST. ALBANS
WRITTEN IN 1486

Pungo 140
WILDERNESS
SYSTEMS

"I am larger and better than I thought.
I did not think I held so much goodness."

– WALT WHITMAN

"The best therapist has fur and four legs."

– AUTHOR UNKNOWN

MEET THE DOGS

3

MACK

Melanie and Jack Steele

Mack loves dog shows and dock diving!

4

COOPER

Stella and Bob White

Cooper, like any great Aussie, is a loyal companion with herding instincts and lots of energy.

6

FIONA AND EMMA

Kim, Lauren and Mark Collins

As invaluable family members, Fiona and Emma bring great joy to the lives of the Collins.

9

GIA

Melanie and Jack Steele

Gia's love of life makes her the consummate entertainer for her family and followers.

10

GRADY

Jeff, Tracy and Macy Schyberg

Grady enjoys a two second break in between his wild runs around the property.

11

RIGBY

Steve and Nancy Sayer

Rigby presents himself as a quiet, dignified gentleman.

12

BOWSER AND SAVANNAH

Sandy and David Boucher

Bowser and Savannah, always the best of friends, enjoy a moment of respite.

13

ARIEL

Ellie Kovalcik

Ariel has a big heart, a bigger personality, and an undying devotion to Ellie, her best friend.

14

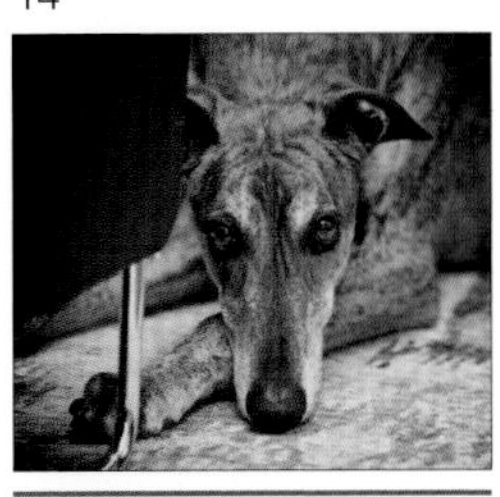

GRANGE

Melanie and Jack Steele

Grange is a stallion-like dog with the spirit of a thoroughbred, the grace of a swan and the heart of a lion.

15

CODY AND DUKE

Laura and Robert Lemenze

Cody and Duke are like two peas in a pod.

16

EDY

Terry and Ray Travaglione

Edy is a spirited Frenchton who is always ready for action.

17

McGEE

Phil and Liz Doetzel

And to think McGee's family wasn't sure if he could swim!

18

GINGER

Carole Hartness and Rick Jones

Newly rescued, Ginger is now filled with a joyful, free spirit of a new life.

19

GRACIE MICHELLE

Jessica and Joel Silverman

Gracie Michelle, like a true Fashionista, strikes a pose.

20

CANDY

Marge and Norm Agin

Candy is like Peter Pan—she never grows old.

22

CHARLIE

Bay and Jeff Lobb

Charlie has his bags packed and is ready to explore exciting new places.

23

CIRRUS

Darlene and John Stang

Cirrus believes that many parts of a pine cone could possibly be edible.

24

LUIGI

Maria and John Brittis

Rescued from the talons of a hawk as a puppy, Luigi is sure that he is now invincible.

MEET THE DOGS

25

LUNA

Eric and Susan Schwelke

Luna loves to run, jump and play with her family.

26

DEUCE AND SMOOCH

Alison and Bill Kimble

Deuce and Smooch are ball chasing buddies.

27

SMOOCH

Alison and Bill Kimble

Smooch is a very inquisitive Yorki Poo.

28

COAL

Judy Harrison and Mike Stepanavage

Coal is equally at home on the beach or on the porch.

29

DAISY AND LEXI

Darren and Terri Karst

Daisy and Lexi are as different as yellow and black, but share a love of food, walks and Palmetto Bluff.

30

DUPREE

Angie Majors and Linda Downs

Dupree is proof that a small package can have tons of life and love inside.

31

LUCY

Caroline and Tyler Filacchione

Lucy performs her puppy version of the moonwalk.

32

EBBI

John and Lynn Tortorici

Ebbi loves to fetch just about anything.

33

JACK DANIELS "DANNY"

Jill and Mark Blitzer

Danny is Master of the Frisbee Have Frisbee, will fly.

34

LUCKY AND HENRY

Sharon and Jim Mattei

Lucky and Henry often have different opinions on the subject.

35

RUSTY AND HARLEY

Sharon and Jim Mattei

Rusty and Harley have gathered their evidence and are ready to hold court.

36

BAILEY

Chris and Scott Dalton

Vocal and vigilant, Bailey is ready to hunt.

37

CHESTER

Anne and Bryan McClure

It has been said that Chester can point on command.

38

MIDGE AND ELLIE

Jack and Susan Robinson

Midge and Ellie find each other's company exhilarating.

39

JAKE

Jim Cunningham

Jake is ready for any adventure with his dad.

40

GUS

Chuck and J.B. Wall

Gus opens the door himself when he wants to swim.

41

ROBEY

Chuck and J.B. Wall

Robey enjoys strolling through Wilson Village.

42

MADIGAN AND CONNOR

Scott and Jackie Evans

Madigan, Connor, Georgia and Emma are beautifully trained, well behaved masters of their universe.

MEET THE DOGS

43

GEORGIA AND EMMA

Scott and Jackie Evans

Madigan, Connor, Georgia and Emma are beautifully trained, well behaved masters of their universe.

45

WILLIAM

Melanie and Jack Steele

William is an old soul with a loving spirit and a zest for life.

46, 47

JASPER

Dana Perino and Peter McMahon

Jasper is America's Dog.

48

BOSCO

Michael and Kelli Ventling

Bosco is the Portie who loves porching.

49

KEH AND SABI

Vikki Bryant

Keh seeks wisdom while Sabi seeks attention.

50

PHOEBE

Geordie and Patricia Cole

Phoebe is Queen of the Dog Park.

51

MALLEY

Malcolm and Julia Butler

Malley goes to work every day with her human parents, serving as their firm's Chief Morale Officer.

52

SADIE

Michael and Sonya Haire

Sadie is small but mighty.

53

LEMON

Sidney Blocker

Lemon is dignified and determined.

54

LOUIS

Pete and Connie Radwanski

Louis is a very proper guy with a sophisticated air about him.

55

PURDEY AND LOUIE

Jacqueline and Jonathan Guarisco

Purdey and Louie give you the sense that they have everything under control.

56

MISS MARLEY MAY

Jane and Howard Grant

When her dad plays the piano, Miss Marley May sings along with a joyful noise.

57

MACALLAN "MAC"

Michael and Joan Daniel

Mac has many tricks in his repertoire which are oftentimes interspersed with short naps.

58

DUDLEY

Gina Daniel

Dudley finds a quiet moment to reflect on the day.

59

MAGGIE

Debbie and Dave Carlucci

As a successful therapy dog, Maggie brings joy and comfort to all those she visits.

60

SANTO

Melanie and Jack Steele

Santo is absolutely sure he is the King of something.

61

MAY DAY, JACK FROST, AND ABIGALE

Gordon and Angela Gale

May Day, Jack Frost and Abigale spend their days in search of other critters to terrorize.

62

ZARA AND ZSA ZSA

C. Parker Cook Jr.

Zara and Zsa Zsa—two partners in crime.

MEET THE DOGS

63

LUCY
Michael Perry
Lucy is always ready, locked and loaded for the hunt.

64

LADY
Cheryl and Robert Twillman
Lady loves boat rides on the May River.

64

MOXIE
Nancy and Tom Frasier
Moxie loves morning walks with her dad and overnights with her brother Mojo.

65

MOJO
Cheryl and Robert Twillman
Mojo is determined to chase every fox squirrel in the Bluff.

65

ZEUS
Cheryl and Robert Twillman
Zeus and pals Moxie and Mojo love to cozy up by the fire.

66

BELLA
Bob and Renee Meighan
Bella is full of life and tricks—from praying mantis to the dancing queen.

67

BYRDIE AND LOLA
Autumn Kirk
Byrdie and Lola are constant companions through thick and thin.

68

LITTLE MAN
Margie Backaus
Little Man and his band of Cavaliers are ready to rumble!

69

ISABELLA, **Alexandra Gewirtz. GEORGINA**, **Joan Gewirtz. WINNIE**, **Jacqueline and Jonathan Guarisco. ANNIE AND HARPER**, **Lee Anne and Bill MacDade. RILEY AND CODY**, **Bob and Danielle Sullivan**
Our cast of Cavaliers—ready for adventure.

70

MADISON
Elizabeth and Jeff Schulte
Madison is the strong, silent type.

71

MADISON, LOLA, AND ANNIE
Mike and Nina Milner
Madison, Lola and Annie are ready for a Road Trip!

72

MAIZE GRACE
Lindsay and Nancy Thomas
Maize Grace can often be found contemplating her afternoon snack at RT's Market.

73

LILLY AND LAYLA
Sandy and David Boucher, Emily and Andrew Ravenna
Though Layla lives in Florida, she enjoys spending time with Lilly when their extended families get together.

74

MARGAUX
Richard and Lacreasa Allen
Margaux prefers the feel of silk against her coat and yodels when she's excited.

75

LUCY AND ROCKY
John and Terri Rosin
Lucy and Rocky love to spend their days riding in a golf cart.

76

MOOSE AND CARTER
Ashleigh McFall
Moose is ready to go but Carter is not sure it's quite time yet.

77

MINNIE PEARL
Judith Redden
Attitude darling! It's all about the attitude. All dressed up and no place to go!

MEET THE DOGS

78

SOPHIE

C. Parker Cook Jr.

Sophie—a dear, tolerant Jack Russell who lives with two wild Chihuahuas.

79

TJ AND MAC

Sharon and Paul Pepe

TJ and Mac love to hang out at the fire pits waiting on s'mores.

80

ROXANNE

Nancy and Paul Fisher

Roxanne loves riding in the car and running in her yard.

81

PIPPA

Sunny Thompson

Pippa lives a life of royalty.

82

RILEY

Kathryn O'Connor

Riley—a steady, faithful companion for over 15 years.

83

OLIVER

Carole Hartness and Rick Jones

Oliver contemplates his good fortune to have been rescued and given a life of love and security.

84

DIXIE

Chris and Scott Dalton

This is Dixie's serious side.

85

SOPHIE AND SAWYER

Glenn and Kim Garby

Sophie and Sawyer are the keepers of their castle.

86, 87

SCOTIA AND SABLE

Trish and Dick Schulze

Sable is a master hunter from Scotland, no less, and Scotia is her best buddy and partner in training.

88

LONGLEAF'S SAM-BO "SAM"

Susan and Charley Tarver

Sam loves retrieving quail to the wagon, retrieving a tennis ball, and jumping in the pool to retrieve anything.

89

SOPHIE AND SIMON BAKER

Mary Kaye and Warner Peacock

Sophie says, "You get it Simon Baker. I went in last time."

90

TACHA

Gary and Kathleen Winer

Tacha—a heart wrapped in fur.

91

PILOT

Mrs. Daryl Hagopian and Mr. Eric Hagopian

Pilot loves treats … lots of treats!

92

WRANGLER

Marge and Norm Agin

Wrangler can be found by following the trail of tennis balls she always carries with her.

93

WILLIAM AND BELLE

Debbie Mast

William and Belle are living the sporting life.

94

BAY

John, Ella, Jack and Gavin Binder

Bay has a gentle spirit and a welcoming expression.

95

TESS

Joe and Linda Mascetti

Tess is wired for sound. No stop … only GO.

97

VERA, GRANGE, AND GIA

Melanie and Jack Steele

The gate keepers.

MEET THE DOGS

MACK

Melanie and Jack Steele

Truffles, what Truffles??? Mack is the original water dog!

RAJAH

Melanie and Jack Steele

Rajah—A prince among men.

BANKS AND MOULTRIE

Brandon W. and Mary Coleman Smith

Banks and Moultrie have been best buddies forever and are the light of their family's life.

INDY AND PICKLES

Stuart and Cathy Malone

Indy and Pickles are doubles partners.

WILSON

Sue Burden

Wilson serves as a floral advisor.

JASPER

Barbara and Mike Blakley

Jasper is a social fellow who loves to visit with folks around The Bluff.

BEHIND THE SCENES

Vera wants Lindsay to know just how much she loves her!

Lindsay, Holli, Melanie and Kathryn grab a few minutes of rest in between the photo shoots.

With two humans in the bed of the truck and one who is trying unsuccessfully to hide behind, this was our most challenging endeavor. The dogs and their humans were a blast to work with! Special thanks to Susan Ketchum for allowing us to borrow "Lola" for this photo. Lola is a 1959 Chevy Apache Fleetside. She is fully restored to her original condition and beautiful "Tartan Turquoise" color that was all the rage that year. She has been part of the Lowcountry since she was purchased from the Sundance Catalog in 2006.

It isn't as easy as it sometimes looks, especially when there are multiple dogs involved.

Hauling a 100 pound Greyhound up two stories into a tree house made for an interesting moment for Lindsay and Melanie.

Tacha also wants Lindsay to know she loves her. Most all of our subjects felt that way about Lindsay.

Riley says, "Seriously, Mom, I don't need the vest or the lead …"